MY

HEAD

IS NOT FOR

SALE

TELLA OLAYERI

TELLA OLAYERI

All rights reserved under International Copyright Law. Content may not be reproduced in whole or in part or in any form without the consent of the publisher.

Email; tellaolayeri@gmail.com
Website tellaolayeri.com.ng

US Contact
Ruth Jack
14 Milewood Road
Verbank
N.Y.12585
U.S.A. +19176428989

APPRECIATION

I give special appreciation to my wife **MRS NGOZI OLAYERI** for her assistance in ensuring that this book is published and our children that play around us to encourage us day and night.

Also, this manuscript wouldn't have seen the light of the day, if not for the spiritual encouragement I gathered from my father in the Lord, **Dr. D.K. OLUKOYA** who served as spiritual mirror that brightens my hope to explore my calling (Evangelism).

We shall all reap our blessings in heaven but the battle to make heaven is not over, until it is won.

PREFACE

This is a deliverance and violent prayer book that addresses the head. The title, "My head is not for sale", says it all. The book gives details of the head and prayer to combat witchcraft powers or self-made problems that may disturb you.

Our head needs prayer to meet God's vision for us. All what we do, all what we need to carry them out are located in the head. That is the reason it is said, whatever happens to the head affects the body. Thus, the chemistry combination of the head must not be allowed to die or affected.

From time of creation to this day, the head is paramount to living. Our Lord fellowshipped with Adam and Eve every evening before the fall of man. Fellowship is done in discussion and on one on one basis. Most of what transpired in fellowship emanates from the eyes, the mouth, and the brain. The signal passed from these outlets, are carried out by other parts of the body.

Today, when you say "My head is not for sale" it means, you shall not be a victim of circumstances. The key to excel is in your hand.

PREVIOUS PUBLICATIONS OF THE AUTHOR

1. *Fire for Fire Prayer Book Part 1*
2. *Fire for Fire Prayer Book Part 2*
3. *Bye Bye to Poverty Part 1*
4. *Bye Bye to Poverty Part 2*
5. *My Marriage Shall Not Break*
6. *Prayer for Pregnant Women*
7. *Prayer for Fruit of the Womb*
8. *Children Deliverance*
9. *Prayer for Youths and Teenagers*
10. *Magnetic Prayer for Singles*
11. *Victory over satanic house Part 1*
12. *Victory over satanic house Part 2*
13. *I Shall Excel*
14. *Atomic Prayer Points*
15. *Goliath at the gate of marriage*
16. *Deliverance from Spirit of Dogs*
17. *Naked warriors*
18. *Power to Overcome Sex in the Dream*
19. *Strange Women! Leave My Husband Alone*

20. *Dangerous Prayer against Strange Women*

21. *Solution to Unemployment*

22. *630 Acidic Prayer Points*

23. *Prayer for Job Seekers*

24. *Power to Retain Job and Excel in Office*

25. *Warfare in the Office*

26. *Power to Overcome Unprofitable Wealth*

27. *Command the Year*

28. *Deliverance Prayer for First Born*

29. *Deliverance Prayer for Good Health and Divine Healing*

30. *Warfare Prayer against Untimely Death.*

31. *Dictionary of Dreams*

32. *Discover Gold and Build Wealth*

33. *My Head is not for Sale*

34. *830 Prophecies for the head*

35. *30 Power Points for the Head*

36. *Prayer after Dreams*

37. *Prayer to Locate Helpers*

38. *Anointing for Eleventh Hour Help*

39. *100% Confessions and Prophecies to Locate Helpers*

40. *Hidden Treasures Exposed!*

41. Prayer to Cancel Bad Dreams

42. Prayer to Remember Dreams

43. 1010 Dreams and interpretations

44. 650 Dreams and Interpretation

45. 1,000 Prayer Points for Children Breakthrough

46. Emergency telephone calls of God

47. I Am Not Alone

48. My Well of Honey shall not dry

49. Shake Heaven with Praises

50 Deliverance prayer for Middle Born Part One

51. 800 Deliverance prayer for Middle Born Part Two

52. Deliverance prayer for Last Born Part One

53. 800 Deliverance prayer for Last Born Part Two

TELLA OLAYERI

Table of Contents

MY HEAD IS NOT FOR SALE 9
FALCULTY OF THE BRAIN 25
FACULTY OF THE MOUTH 50
FACULTY OF THE EYE 60
FACULTY OF THE EAR 77
WHEN THE HEAD NEEDS DELIVERANCE 85

CHAPTER ONE

MY HEAD IS NOT FOR SALE

Brethren, before we read this topic, bless your head in poem like prayer below.

I am the HEAD and not the tail
My head is anointed with anointing of favour
Mercy and peace are mine
Because I am the head and not the tail

I shall not be relegated to the background
Spells shall not locate my head
Wasters shall not waste me
Arrows of darkness shall not locate me
Because I am the head and not the tail

Tail region is not my portion
I am created to occupy mountain top
My peers shall have cause to respect me
They shall look unto me as a leader
Because I am the head and not the tail

The hair on my head is uncountable
It is like sand in the seashore
Favour of God upon me is countless
Mercy of God upon me is immeasurable
I shall be a goal-getter anywhere I go
Because I am the head and not the tail

The Glory of the Lord is upon me
Men and women shall favour me
Attacks are far from me
Enemies shall bow before me
Because I am the head and not the tail

From the above poem, we can see that our head is a prominent part of the body. It plays vital role in our life.

Brethren, before we go further, let's quickly define what is meant by head. Head is the upper region of the body that rests on the neck. The head is divided into precisely defined components, each with specific function. The head defines one on recognition from far or at close range by ones face.

The head is the power-house of existence. No human being goes about without a head on his neck. It is possible to do without other parts of the body, but it is impossible to go about without a head. For example one can lose an eye, or lose both, and still move about. You can do without your ears, lips, teeth, jaw or hair, but then you can't do without the head. You may lose both legs and arms, and be alive, but once the head is cut off, death is the ultimate. This is the reason, the head is important in human chemistry.

The head is a symbol of existence. In the battle field, enemies target the head of opponents. If other parts of the body are shot, there may be a chance of survival, but where the head is shot or cut off, survival is remote. When David killed Goliath, he was not too sure or satisfied until he drew his sword and cut his head. It was at this point, he was satisfied that Goliath was dead. No wonder, commanders in the battle field says, "Aim the head of opponent at war".

The use of the word head is both figurative and biological. Figurative description foretells statements like, the head of state, the head of the family, the head of a group, head of a committee, head of a gang etc. These classes of heads mean leadership. For example, men are regarded as head of the house. The fact is, no marriage is storm-free without the head. A man is joined in marriage from a different home, different background, different philosophy, different financial set up etc. As the head of the house, a man needs healing and anointing to cope with situations as they arise.
Biological head is that part of human body, called human head. Each creature that breathe with nose, either animal or ant have a head. But then, what we shall discuss here is human head. It has about thirteen parts, starting from the hair to the neck region that divides it from other parts of the body. The parts are mentioned as follows:
1. Hair
2. Forehead
3. Eyebrow

4. Bridge
5. Temple
6. Eye
7. Ear
8. Cheek
9. Nose
10. Nostril
11. Mouth
12. Jaw
13. Chin.

The head is a masterpiece of invention, creativity, wisdom and knowledge. It is also, warehouse magnet of favour and mercy. You must have idea to boost your dream, goal and potential. To realize this, you must develop potentials in you. The potentials, start from the head. The potential is like seed planted in you.

There is a seed in you that must be discovered and nurtured for growth; an idea to discover, and nurture. It all starts from the head. This seed must germinate and grow to become a big tree of fruition. No wonder it is said, "There is a giant tree in every seed". The fact remains there is a woman in a girl. There is a man in a little boy. There is a giant successful company in little ideas you start with. It is a tragedy for a giant in you to die premature death.

It is therefore a must to build on gifts God deposited in you. The gifts from the Lord are door openers for great men and women. The Bible says, **"A gift opens the way for the giver and ushers him into the presence of the great" Proverbs 18:16.** Thus opportunities and breakthroughs start from the head. Your potential is dominant ability to forge ahead. It is the youth energy inside of you, the reserved power wanting to be activated. Apply and make use of every deposit in you, as the world is waiting when you will be of use to them. Your potential is in you. It is a divine deposit. Apply what you have to actualize it.

Your potential is your hidden power. To be born again doesn't mean that the deposit in you shall wake; it is you that must go into action. It is therefore necessary to pray ideas in you into life and manifestation. Hence, you should pray against powers that may cage you.

Your potential is the sleeping giant in you that has power to grow. It is an ability yet to be realized. When the head is delivered, the greatness in a person appears, while doors of blessings open. The reason is, that the uniqueness in you shall manifest to produce unique product, as there is no duplicate of you anywhere in the world.

On this premise, you need mercy and favour of God and of men. Your head must attract goodness. When you have right contact, the Lord adds value to it. When anointing of God is upon you, what seems difficult for others becomes simple to you.

Darkness stirs clear of at you, while light of God shines on you. Instead of being messed up, you become talk of the town. It becomes impossible for enemies to carry out their mission against you or turn you upside down.

You can develop the potentials in you if only you are able to identify or know potential killers around you. God knew there are potential killers around us. There are demons ready to feed us, attack our well-being and our head in particular. As a person, you should fight back in the manner and attitude of, "I shall not surrender my destiny to the wind".

The fact is, if you fail to know and kill anti-potential killers, they will master you, and kill you. To avoid this, you must act and say it in clear language, "My head is not for sale"

When you say, "My head is not for sale", it is more than what eyes can see and what ears can hear. It is a statement loaded with meanings.

When you say, "My head is not for sale", it means divine anointing is upon you. What it means in essence is; your destiny is on line favoured, it is multi-geographically favoured, it is linguistically favoured, and it is multi-currency favoured, with real access time favour. In a nut-shell, it means you are favoured all round in life.

To say, "My head is not for sale", is a claim of crown of gold on the head. What you mean is; you are a leader not a servant, the head and not the tail. You are saying, you are a person of recognition. You are saying, you are crowned with crown of blessings, as written in the book of **Proverbs 10:6, "Blessings crown the head of the righteous"** It is a claim of someone loaded with assurance of salvation. You are save because helmet of salvation is on your head. What you are saying is, your head is not a candidate for insults and that no disgrace shall locate you.

When you say, "My head is not for sale", it is a statement of dominion over nature, and creation, and every contrary power around you. It means, God made you dominion over all creation. It is a declaration that, you are not created to serve powers that emanates from creation. It is a statement of liberty over creation.

When you say "My head is not for sale", it is a prophetic claim of right to be taller than others. To be taller than others, mean to be recognized for wisdom, knowledge and understanding. It means to have upper hand in the midst of peers.

When you say, "My head is not for sale", you are announcing to the world that you are created to occupy the head region, not the tail region of life. You are saying your destiny cannot be rubbished. You are saying, you won't be dragged from the front roll of life to occupy the back sit of life. It means, you shall be recognized anywhere you go. You mean, helpers shall see and recognize you for help. Hence, you shall not be turned down.

When you say, "My head is not for sale", it means your destiny is protected. Jacob must have said this several times beyond understanding of Esau. Right in the womb, he wrestled with his brother, Esau for headship. When they were born, Esau lost to Jacob. The claim of Jacob superseded Esau.

To say, "My head is not for sale", is not an ordinary statement, but a claim of breakthrough above poverty and stagnation. It is a statement of match against poverty that foretells success, joy and breakthrough. It is a safe way of saying, "I am a lender to nations, and never shall I borrow before I feed". You claim self-sufficiency and ability to go extra mile to help others. Thus, it is a claim that you are not a non-entity but one to be reckoned with. When Jabez discovered that he was in a wrong position of life, he cried in the manner of, "O Lord, my head (destiny) is in wrong hands and in a wrong place, help me, my head is not for sale; enlarge my coast by fire".

To say "My head is not for sale", is a cry against bad health. It is a claim that you are not a candidate of clinics and hospitals, and that; your household is neither one as well. It is a way of thanking God, in the like, "O Lord, thank you for good health that reigns in my family"
When you say "My head is not for sale", it is a pre-warning statement that the use of head factors, like the eyes, ear, mouth etc. shall not work against you. The eyes of Esau put him in everlasting problem. His eyes saw porridge, his mouth pronounced the sale of his birth right. All these emanates from the brain. Thus, his eyes, his mouth and his brain all located in the head region engineered the sale of his birth right.

When you say "My head is not for sale", it is a prophetic statement of vision. It is a claim that your vision shall not die. It is a claim that God shall open your inner eyes for great adventure. It is a statement of having BIG DREAM. It is a statement of abundance. Big dreams are products of sound brain, of deep knowledge and wisdom.

When you say "My head is not for sale", it means it shall not be shaved in disgrace in the order of

Samson at the mercy of Delilah. You are saying you are a symbol of greatness and that your glory shall not be tampered with. You are saying no strange razor or strange power shall shave your head as a result of dream attack.

To these, it can be safely said, the head is a delicate part of the body that must be jealously guided. Whatever affects the head, affect the whole body as well. Caution must be applied whenever something is to be applied on the head. You must be aware of what it contains and the effects as well.

We must note it is only God who is a destiny repairer. We often leave him aside and seek help elsewhere. This is the reason; you must not surrender your head or that of your children for incision or apply concoction on them. The foundation of such power is demonic and ungodly.

One must take caution to follow people that parade themselves as men of God. Many are wolves in sheep clothing. You may think they are genuine but they are fakes. The anointing oil which most of them apply on counselees is demonic. Once the anointing oil is applied, victim loses focus and is hypnotized. This is the reason you don't run after men of God you can't vouch for, so that your head is not rubbed with oil of sorrow. A rush after them by some people caused them fatal spiritual accidents in the race of life.

At this junction, you have two options to address. Your situation is to first take your destiny before God, who happens to be our destiny repairer. He is the King of kings, and Lord of lords. He is the only one who can lift our head above friends and contemporaries, above Satan and his agents, and above living and non-living objects or powers. He is the divine healer and head washer. He can heal every manner of diseases or sickness, undiluted, unequal and permanent. If God washes your head, you become a new being, you will experience new anointing, new strength and new vision. If your head experience heavenly repair, afflictions and iniquities shall vanish in your life. Every manner of curse pronounced against you shall cease. Power of stagnancy and failure troubling your soul shall expire. You shall experience heavenly support and attention, while those who hate you before now, shall become friends, because the Lord is on your side.

The second option is to pray on anointing oil by injecting it with blood of Jesus or soak it in blood of Jesus. Hence, you command blood of Jesus to flow into it for signs and wonders. Raise it to the Almighty God for acceptance and power. Anoint your head with it, and tell God what you want. Therefore, command all manner of problems on your head to come out by fire and die. Command evil arrows fired against you to come out and go back to sender. Command evil deposit in your head to be uprooted to its root. Command evil plantations to wither to their roots and die.

Be spirit filled, whatever you say will be recorded in heaven.

Whatever you bind here on earth, shall be bound in heaven.

Whatever you lose here on earth, shall it be loosed in heaven.

Whenever you break powers of stronghold troubling your head here, so shall it be in heaven.

Whenever you command wicked powers to scatter by fire, so shall it be in heaven.

When you command wicked powers and their activities to catch fire and roast to ashes so shall it be.

When you fire back evil arrow so shall it be as well.

Therefore, mean what you say, and expect result. Develop yourself, don't be a baby Christian, waiting to be fed with the Word every day. You are a gallant soldier of Christ, loaded with spiritual bullets and ammunitions. Stop being fed with milk all the time; learn to be a prayerful giant. Eat solid spiritual food that will strengthen you. Don't go after fake men of God that wash glory of men into the sea, river or stream, calling it deliverance. Your mouth can deliver you in prayer and fasting.

Many heads so washed are dying out fast. They experience multiple doze of problems. Instead of getting solution to their problems, they run into one problem or the other, as their heads are decorated with medals of calamities. No wonder, such people saw themselves carrying evil load in the dream. As if this is not enough, they are harassed sexually in the dream or fed with demonic food. All these make them experience failure at the edge of breakthrough. They are kept in chains by fake pastors that smile to the bank with ill-gotten wealth. The fact is, these fake pastors need deliverance. They can be likened to a deliverer that needs deliverance.

It is high time you break every covenant of failure associated with your head. Cleanse your head with blood of Jesus. Claim your destiny that is sold to the wind. Release yourself from friends that mock you and your family. What more?, cleanse your head of evil lice that feast on it. They are powers that suck blood, eat flesh of victims and introduce poverty to life. Such powers should die. This you can do with prayers.
Now let's pray.

PRAYER POINTS

1. Anointing of God upon my head shall not dry in the name of Jesus

2. Mercy and peace locate me by fire in the name of Jesus

3. I shall be the head and not the tail, in the name of Jesus

4. Every power of waster assigned to waste my life, die in the name of Jesus

5. Every arrow of darkness fired against me, backfire in the name of Jesus

6. My head in the market of darkness, be released in the name of Jesus

7. Divine favour!, my head is available for you, enter, in the name of Jesus

8. My head! You are the symbol of my destiny; enemy shall not conquer you, in the name of Jesus.

9. My head shall not be anchored to failure in the name of Jesus

MY HEAD IS NOT FOR SALE

10. My head shall not be anchored to sickness in the name of Jesus

11. I cut off the head of my enemy that wants to cut off my head in the name of Jesus

12. Goliath! Boasting against my David, die in the name of Jesus

13. Whatever healing my head lacks, receive the healing today, in the name of Jesus

14. Great inventions deposited in my head, manifest, in the name of Jesus

15. Seed of greatness planted in my life germinate in the name of Jesus

16. My head receive energy, forge ahead, in the name of Jesus

17. My head, receive fire deliverance today, in the name of Jesus

18. Potentials in me shall not die, in the name of Jesus

19. My head, possess potential of leadership, in the name of Jesus

20. O Lord, crown my head with crown of blessings, in the name of Jesus

21. My head, be loaded with wisdom, knowledge and understanding in the name of Jesus

22. Abundance of wealth, locate my head, in the name of Jesus

23. Powers of darkness assigned to share my head, die in the name of Jesus

24. Strange razor assign against my hair, break to pieces, in the name of Jesus

25. Power of incision upon my head, die, in the name of Jesus

26. Concoction of darkness applied on my head, causing havoc in my life, I cleanse you with blood of Jesus

27. I shall not lose focus, in the race of life, in the name of Jesus

28. Fake anointing oil applied on my head by fake pastors, dry up and seize to affect me wrongly, in the name of Jesus

29. Stronghold of darkness upon my life, scatter in the name of Jesus

CHAPTER TWO

FALCULTY OF THE BRAIN

The brain is mostly divided into three parts: the cerebrum, the cerebellum, and the medulla oblongata. Most decisions in life are taken in the brain. While some are quite automatic, others are made only after careful consideration. Human brain is crucial to thinking and decision making. The brain is like an automatic guidance system, which steer life towards realization of the mental self-image fed into it. No wonder medical experts warned against dangers of allowing the brain to experience infection, disorder or disease.

As good as brain is, so are human intelligence varies. And this matter, because smarter people generally earn more money, enjoy better health, raise smarter children, feel happier and, live longer as well.

There are more to the brain as we see it. But before we go into details of the brain, we may ask, what do we mean by this five letter words, called brain? In simple term, brain is the mass of soft grey matter in the head Centre of the nervous system. The human brain is 70% water. It is a complex organ, housed in the skull. Without brain, the body is entirely useless, while human activity becomes meaningless.

How can we define brain? It is the organ of memory, reasoning, intelligence and understanding. Without the brain we are useless. This is because the ability to remember is one of our most important assets, without it, we are hopelessly lost and confuse.

What do we mean by the word brain? It is the mind leader, while mind is the workshop of assets. All what you become originates from the brain.

Let's ask again, what do we mean by the word brain? It is the seat of our thought processes. It is the organ responsible for consciousness, self-examination and inquiry. It is when you are able to do self-audit you can know where you are heading to in life. When you see wrong signal ahead, you dodge it and cry out and shout in the like, 'My head is not for sale'.

What do we mean by the word brain? It is the machine like nature of the body: it keeps the body moving.

What is brain? The brain is that part of the body in the head that is able to remember, and also to learn.

May we ask again, what do we mean by brain? It is the source of intellectual power. The brain composes our thinking faculty. All thinking takes place in the brain. It is the seat of our thought processes. It is the organ responsible for consciousness, self-examination and enquiry. The brain is the source of our intellectual power.

It is in the brain and brain alone, arise our pleasures, joys and laughter and jests, as well as our sorrows, pains, grieves, and tears. It is this same brain that make us mad, inspires us with dread and fear, whether by day or by night. Our sleepless nights, mistakes and errors made, aimless anxieties, absent mindedness and acts that are contrary to habit originate from the brain.

The brain is just one part of the nervous system; together with the spinal cord it forms the **Central Nervous System (CNS).** With brain we are able to remember and also to learn.

The brain is the memory power house. Our memory makes us understand what we see, feel, touch or hear. It also helps to transmit our ideas to other people. Basically, we have two types of memory; temporal and permanent memory. For instance, many times a day, we have to remember certain things such as when to get up, what to buy, where to work, and when to go to bed. Such memories may last only a few minutes. They are more or less temporal. Once we attend to those matters we forget about it. On the other hand, permanent memories are in the like of our name, age, sex, home address, and nationality. Such memories remain with us all the time.

It should however be noted that most of these memories are formed in childhood, or perhaps after some important events. That is why it is very necessary for a child to be well fed with nutritious food and exclusively breast feed at least for the next six months to one year of life, so that, such child can have better brain development that will ensure better Intelligence Quotient (IQ)

The greatest and most complex computer one can think of in this world is the brain. It is said to contain about 100 billion nerve cells that begin to die at birth. Imagine your tiny head having 100 billion brain nerve cells. These nerve cells form in shape to improve and increase sense growth. The brain has two major parts of roles in the body; the conscious and the sub-conscious. In human activities, the conscious mind controls and guides the sub-conscious mind.

The brain is with verse cells that can be said to be uncountable. It is an instrument of such incalculable capabilities that one engineer has estimated it would take a building several acres in size to house the computers that would match the dullest human brain! And at that, you would have the world's smartest man-made computer; it would still lack the self- input generating power that every human being possesses.

Among those billions of cells in the brain, there lie thousands of brilliant but slumbering cells that are charged with vast powers waiting to be aroused, harnessed, and unleashed. If you can discover a way to stimulate them; you will be amazed at your own brilliance and intelligence. This is the reason you must guide against anything that may affect your brain. It is the powerhouse that brings wealth of glory, comfort and joy. Therefore, you must not allow dark powers to advertise or sell your brain in the spirit.

There are billions of nerves in the brain that makes it operate fast. The fast operational value of nerves makes it to be called the 'great analyzer'. The number of connections within one human brain rivals the number of stars and galaxies in the universe and far exceeds the human population of our planet.
There are motor and sensory nerves that are connected to different parts of the brain. Specific region of the brain perform specific functions. Mental processes occur in cells of the brain. Without good connectivity of nerves in the brain, learning process would be impossible because information is passed between the nerve cells.

Some years ago a wise man who wrote most of the Psalms said in the first book of Psalms, ***"The blessed man is like a tree planted by the rivers of water, bringing forth fruit every season. Its leaf never withers and everything he touches seems to prosper"*** The blessed man is the man whose brain functions well. Out of the treasures of wisdom in him, he lacks nothing but bring forth fruit every season. Its leaves never wither; means its branches are good and healthy. Thus, the cells that make brain function well are source of prosperity and breakthrough.

A CASE STUDY

Wisdom emanates in the head, the brain of course. But then, we must be cautious of information we receive and how we apply them, as such advert may be dangerous. The story was said of a T.V. Star. Some years back, for many years the most famous of the early newscasters on television was sponsored by Chesterfield cigarettes. He would conclude his news program by lighting up a cigarette, while the name of the brand was on the screen. He immediately relaxed. The image of peace was so vivid that the sales of Chesterfields increased enormously and boosted the profits of the company

It was later told that when the broadcaster was dying of lung cancer, and struggling for every breath, he asked to appear on the same TV program so that others might see the long term results of what he had previously advertised. His request was refused. He died!

A man or woman with good brain prospers; anything he or she touches prospers as well. Therefore, you are expected to avoid whatever may endanger your brain, and say, "Leave my head alone, my head is not for sale"

The brain is the power house of wisdom. When brain is affected, the head and mind are affected as well. When brain faculty is sound, the mind improves. All is well, because wisdom takes place in the brain. The book of ***James 1:15, says, "If any of you lack wisdom, he should ask God, who gives generously to all without finding fault, and it will be given to him"***.

When you study the Bible, call for power of Holy Spirit for understanding, knowledge and wisdom. Your quiet time with God opens room for wisdom. In the book of John 8:26, the Ethiopian rich man read the script but couldn't understand but for Philip who guided him with the help of the Holy Spirit. Pray to God for sound knowledge so that you may fulfill your destiny. Don't sell your ideas to the wind, if you do, it equates selling your head. Be firm and say, "My head is not for sale".

Brain is a thinking powerhouse. Most initiatives, actions, and directives originate in the brain. Once the brain is tampered with, disorder takes place. To have a troubled brain is dangerous mostly when it relates to insanity. An insane person is avoided by people. His behavior and acts don't go well with people. His thinking faculty is questionable. He needs attention and grace.

Today, many are depressed because they overtax the brain, trying to follow a daily routine that is beyond their mental, emotional and physical resources. Brain stress, couple with negative thoughts and emotions, affect the body and contribute a chemical imbalance in the brain, producing depression. The book of **Proverbs 14:30 says, "A heart at peace gives life to the body but envy rots the bones"** Envy originates from the head through the eyes that see and, ear that hears. Such message is transferred to the brain, which leads to decision. If a message is received with envy, it can lead to negative thought to kill, cheat or harm. Such brain works other way round for evil.

The brain is such a special asset to mankind. Whoever tries to waste your brain is a killer. Insanity is rampant this day as a result of manmade problems and attacks from strange source and powers.

A CASE STUDY

Attack can be spiritual or physical. Some years back a brother had repeated dreams of a police officer that hit his head with baton. He said the spirit police officer look like a giant and very fearful. Anytime this brother dreamt of this officer who tortures him with several hits of baton on the head he woke into severe headache. Not only this, he experience failure at the edge of breakthrough as well. Things don't work out as planned, as he was arrested with fear and heartache. As a result he lacks connecting spirit to co-ordinate activities.

Your brain regulates your composition and spirit. Anything that affects your brain affects you. This is the reason enemies target the head. Attack on the head is attack on the brain. Hence, you should be violent in prayer against powers that target you for destruction.

Is your case likened to this brother? If so, you should pray fire prayers. Apply prayers that command heavenly powers to arrest and kill dark security officer that torments you. Command heavenly fire in the order of Elijah, to burn to ashes every dark baton assign against you. Command thunder of God to strike down every strongman assigned against you. Command power of paralysis to strike such power down by fire. Therefore you can pray in this manner:

1. Heavenly thunder, strike down strong man or woman assign to torment me in the name of Jesus.

2. My father, my father, break into pieces evil baton assign against my head in the dream in the name of Jesus.

3. Fire of paralysis; paralyze strongman assign against me in the dream in the name of Jesus

4. Every embargo placed upon my head, break in the name of Jesus.

5. Arrow of God, strike down strongman of my soul to death, in the name of Jesus.

Your potentials are in your brain. You should develop your brain to bring the best out of you. The brain is the internal mirror of the body. If the mirror breaks, body chemistry works in vain. Any power that targets your brain is out to foment cruelty on you. Any power assigned to kill your potentials, aim at killing your brain. When the brain is affected, backwardness and stagnancy set in.

The Bible says, every tree my father has not planted shall be uprooted. Enemies can plant poverty in a head; they can plant affliction in a head as well. They can turn a head into dustbin of life; thereby deposit contrabands and wastes in such life.

How can you know when you are so attacked? Let's answer this from spiritual angle. If you can memorize the Bible before, but now you can't do so, it means your head is most likely to be under attack. Inability to read the Word as you do before is attack on the brain. If you can't meditate on the Word, your brain is under attack. At this point, cry to God in prayer to neutralize, liquidate and destroy contrabands and works of darkness in your life. Let your brain become store house for the Word, so that you can address situation as it arises.

DRUGS AND THE BRAIN

Question that may come to mind is, ***why do people drink, eat, inhale, smoke or inject their body with what is dangerous to the body and brain?*** This is a question yet to receive positive answer.

A CASE STUDY

Some years back as I entered the gate of one University in my country a young boy ran and was pursued by a woman. This woman was in her average age of about 43 years old. When you look at her dress, there is no doubt that she was wealthy and educated.

But as she ran after this young boy shouting, "Help me hold him! Help me hold him! He is my son. Please help me hold him". Passerby couldn't as the boy resisted every attempt to hold him. At this point he was not lucky enough as he fell. He was trapped down like a baby, until her mother arrived, breathing profoundly and crying.
"What is the matter about"? people asked. She narrated it all, without missing word. The boy was an undergraduate of the institution but was involved in drugs. A once brilliant boy became a nuisance in school. Sign of insanity shows in his speech and behavior

At first, he denied ever knowing his mother! As he said, "Who are you? I don't know you" Her mother cried and wept the more. She knelt down begged her son for a change of mind.

All the while, his son was in another frequency. He was loaded in drugs! I later learnt that he ran mad and couldn't complete his education.

I pray, your children shall not fall victim of drugs in the name of Jesus. Amen

It is disturbing to watch men and women getting stoned to drugs especially **Indian hemp.** This drug called India hemp has different names in many cultures and environment. It is called *cannabis,*

stone, grass, pot, ganja, Mary Jane, shunk, lala, Igbo etc. It is smoked by millions of people in the world and usage has escalated even in the face of severe penalties. It is no more products of street urchins, touts and the never-do-well. This day, situation has change as respectable professionals are involved. Many university graduates indulge in the use of the drug as if they also earned degrees in hemp consumption. They wrap it in sizes by names, **Fella, Peter Tosh, Bob Marley, J.J.C, Smalley** etc. the biggest size often goes for Fella.

Dominant reasons for taking it are curiosity, bravado and desire for its effects, which include euphoria, increased sensory awareness and a feeling of well-being. This drug with scientific name *cannabis sativa* has been used through history in many cultures to change mood, perception and consciousness to get high. Its effects among consumers range from increasing creativity, to mystical experiences, to heightening the capacity to feel sense. Where is the origin of this drug? Its origin can be traced to China in the 600BC where its seeds were used severally for food and medicine.

Research reveals that marijuana affects the central nervous system by attaching to the brains neurons. These nerves respond by altering their behavior. For example, if the nerve is supposed to assist one in retrieving short-term memory, carnabiniods receptors make them do the opposite. It has negative effect on users. So if someone has to remember what he did five minutes ago, after smoking a high dose of marijuana, he will have trouble remembering.

Scientists say marijuana plant contains 400 chemicals and 40 of them are cannabinoids which are psycho active components that are produced inside the body after cannabis is metabolized. Cannabinoids is on active ingredient of marijuana. The most psychoactive cannabinoids chemical of marijuana that has the biggest impact on the brain is tetrahydrocanni: bol THC. Psychiatrists, who treat schizophrenic patients, advice not to use this drug; because, it can trigger severe mental disturbance and cause a fall back into bad ways. Don't forget the saying; "The extent you permit devil is the extent you go with him". Hence, I advise you don't journey with drug.

Science has proved that only three percent of the human brain is utilized. With this, you don't need drugs or alcohol to achieve something in life. Since the brain is underutilized, those things are not necessary.

The brain is so important that an injury to a part of it can lead to paralysis of muscles, paralysis of the head, paralysis of the leg etc., and or, disturbance of language *aphasia*, because the muscles responsible for speech production are affected. Speech is low and labored. The speech may sound quite normal, but it lacks content and may incorporate incorrect words.

In 1861, the French physician Pierre-Poul Broca recognized that damage to a specific region of the brain resulted in a language disturbance. This region in the brain is called Broca's area.

Brain damage can affect vision, reading ability, body image etc. At this point, when victim looks at a letter, it seems unfamiliar and foreign to him. It may well be safe to assert that we should regard some forms of brain damage as a first installment of death. It is a rage; it is abortion of the brain that 'vegetabilize' the helpless.

UNKNOWN POWERS AND THE BRAIN

Our brain is made to add value to life, but circumstance made it to be affected by unknown powers. Our environment is loaded with and controlled by wicked forces. They cause pains and fears. Power of unknown causes marital turbulence, confusion, attack on career and calling which affects the brain.

What is this power, called ***power of unknown***? A popular late musician in my country defined it as a social-political factor in his album titled Unknown Soldier. He sang among other things that we have

Unknown Soldier, we have Unknown Police, we have Unknown Civilian, which is equal to Unknown Government. But then it is as if, he lived in analogue age. This age is digital age, things multiply at accelerated speed. Too many things this day include **unknown gunmen, unknown assassins, unknown terrorists, unknown rapists, unknown bombers, unknown fraudsters, unknown kidnappers,** unknown this and unknown that, affects the brain. They are too numerous to count!

When bombarded with the unknowns, the brain is affected. It is more pronounced when citizens of a country blessed with mineral resources and manpower turn to scavengers and beggars on the street. It is a doom and calamity on a country where few loot the treasury, and are treated as sacred cows. What an irony? The sacred cows milk the people dry, but do not produce milk for people's consumption. Rather than build industries to cater for millions unemployed population youths roaming the streets, they starched their stolen wealth to different accounts overseas.

They scatter destines of helpless souls and trade them to the wind. They turn to slave masters that want people to dress poor, eat poor and earn nothing as if they say, ""We have sold your head to the wind". But I encourage you to refute it and say, "My head is not for sale"

I pray that every effort of the wicked to sell your head to the wind shall fail, in the name of Jesus. Amen.

MUSIC AND THE BRAIN

There are wonders music plays in human body and brain in particular. Here, we may quickly ask, what is music to the brain?

Anytime you listen to music, it causes brain to release dopamine which is a feel-good chemical. Whenever you listen to tunes that move you, your brain releases dopamine, a chemical involved in both motivation and addiction.

Music helps with pain management. It helps to ward off depression, promotes movement, calms patients, and eases muscles tension.

Music has a strong beat that stimulates the brain waves, which also affects breathing and heart rate. Trying to listen to some music has been discovered to lower blood pressure and boost immunity. For example, slower music brings slower breathing, and a slower heart rate brings an activation of relaxation response. Thus, music can help counteract or prevent the damaging effects of chronic stress and can bring a more positive state of mind, which affects the brain.

Music entertains you especially after working hours. It is the best 'medicine' for your tired brain, as it sometimes help to eliminate stress and pressure. Everyone, after working or studying really needs music to refill their power.

Music is the reflection of our emotions. It is a good friend that gently heals the soul. When you feel alone or upset, you can listen to your favourite songs and feel better. Music affects sensation and feelings. This can be seen from the roots of the kinds of music we listen to. Rock music was created mostly to reflect anger, whereas ballads must have come out of romantic love stories, or from a painful heart. When you experience what is unpleasant let music divert your mind from this situation.

Music alleviates insomnia. Do you have problems with sleeping? Listening to music soothes your nerves. You drift off to sleep and get the rest needed since sleep puts your body in a healthy condition. This also takes away the effects of stress, depression and anxiety from you, which your brain needs.

MUSIC TO CHOOSE FROM

On the Nigeria music scene, we have music like Afro beat, Juju, Apala, Fuji, Highlife and Gospel.

These are music most people listen to. There is the foreign music genre with various categories such as the Classical, Jazz, Blues, Rock, Hip-hop, and Country music.

The bottom line is, not every genre of music goes with your personality. You should be able to differentiate between bad and good music, what may lead one to hell fire or heaven, or aggravate the mind for lust. As a Christian, listen to gospel music that makes you think heaven. Listen to music that attracts goodness to soul and polish the heart. You are always in your closet when you listen to your favourite music, therefore watch yourself. It is therefore left to you, to identify which music suits you most. You can have different tunes for different moods. Doing this, helps to steady your consciousness and increase your mental organization.

A very good fact is that music influences blood circulation, pulse rate, breathings as well as sweating. It affects the body temperature. Transcendent music can flood you with warmth, while loud music with a strong beat can make your body heat rise a few degrees, while soft music with a weak beat can lower it.

Very close to music is dance. As you sing and listen to music learn to dance too. Dancing has a lot of mental, spiritual and physical benefits.

Dancing is a way to praise and glorify God. But then, we must note here that, **dancing in the modern sense of a social activity between men and women is unknown in the Bible**. It is not encouraged because it aggravates lust.

Dancing prevents Alzheimer's disease and vascular dementic. The need to learn and remember numerous dance movements produce a constant and very beneficial challenge to the brain. Mental intelligence comes from mental exercise and this applies to every one of all ages.

POWER OF DOMINION

God gave us reasoning faculty to have dominion over creation. He gave us brain to excel in what we do. He empowers us to jettison poverty, backwardness and stagnancy over the board in the course of our journey in life. We are created to lead, not servants of creation.

But then, there are powers that want us to be slaves or paupers in their hands. These powers are faceless and don't want victims to excel in life. They attack destinies via head and the brain. They turn thinking faculty of men shallow and unproductive. They kill, and make use of skulls and brain of victims in the spirit. They poison victims in the spirit, and or, do so in the physical.

MY HEAD IS NOT FOR SALE

After a time, victims experience movement of strange objects in their body and the head.

In the long run, if a victim is not prayerful enough or fail to go for deliverance, he may experience brain disorder in the form of persistent headache, migraine, forgetfulness, senseless talk, aggression of mind etc.

Whatever affects the thinking faculty of a person, affect his brain. When you say, "My head is not for sale", you mean, your brain is far from evil attacks. It means your brain is void of sale in the spirit. It means your brain or head shall not experience arrow of darkness. It means your head is not under curse. It means your head is not under padlock of darkness. It means your head is not candidate of evil clinical prophecy. It means your destiny shall not be buried.

I pray that your head and that of your household shall not be under any form of captivity in the name of Jesus. Amen.

At this point I enjoin we go into personal deliverance prayer. Now let's pray.

PRAYER POINTS
1. Owner of evil load, carry your load by fire in the name of Jesus.

2. Evil padlock assign against my brain break to pieces.

3. Lord Jesus, lay your healing hands upon my head for perfect healing.

4. My brain, experience sharp memory in the name of Jesus.

5. I shall not run mad in the name of Jesus.

6. Witchcraft market in charge of my brain, release my brain and catch fire in the name of Jesus.

7. My brain is immuned against attack in the name of Jesus.

8. Heavenly wisdom, fill my brain in the name of Jesus.

9. My brain, manifest breakthrough and success in the name of Jesus

10. Any power assign to suck my brain die in the name of Jesus.

11. .Evil load on my head, fall off and catch fire in the name of Jesus.

12. I rub my head with blood of Jesus to neutralize and destroy effects of evil load, in the name of Jesus.

13. Holy Ghost fire, purify my head, in the name of Jesus

14. My brain, receive deliverance in the name of Jesus

15. I recover my lost glory by fire in the name of Jesus

16. Blood of Jesus flow through my brain in the name of Jesus.

17. My father, my father, deliver me from evil powers in the name of Jesus.

18. Evil thoughts in my brain expire in the name of Jesus.

19. Any power assign to manipulate my brain, die in the name of Jesus.

20. Every fetish power assign against my head, die by fire in the name of Jesus.

21. Evil plantation on my head, die to your root, in the name of Jesus

22. Enemy of my head! You are a failure; die in the name of Jesus.

23. Power of wasters assign against my head, die in the name of Jesus

24. I release my brain from witchcraft cage in the name of Jesus

25. Arrow of memory failure fired against me, backfire and consume your sender in the name of Jesus.

26. Every evil hand placed upon my head, wither by fire in the name of Jesus.

27. Evil transfer on my head as a result of evil hands laid upon me, die in the name of Jesus.

28. Satanic pollution on my head clear away in the name of Jesus

29. Any power attacking my dream life, die in the name of Jesus.

30. Evil materials laid on my head catch fire and roast to ashes in the name of Jesus

31. Every foundational problem troubling my brain die in the name of Jesus.

32. Satanic deposits in my brain dry up in the name of Jesus.

33. Spirit of forgetfulness, I cast you out of my head in the name of Jesus.

34. Spirit of frustration I cast you out of my head in the name of Jesus.

35. Spirit of madness, I cast you out of my head in the name of Jesus.

36. Spirit of brain damage, I cast you out of my head in the name of Jesus.

37. Spirit of brain cancer, I cast you out of my head in the name of Jesus.

38. Spirit of tumor, I cast you out of my head in the name of Jesus.

39. Spirit of confusion, I cast you out of my head in the name of Jesus.

40. Spirit of headache and migraine, I cast you out of my head in the name of Jesus.

CHAPTER THREE

FACULTY OF THE MOUTH

Mouth is the opening through which we eat or talk. It is that part of the body that houses the tongue and teeth. Good as the mouth is, it is essential to note what goes into the stomach through it. Many fell victim of circumstances because they ate in wrong places, talk in wrong places or take food from wrong hands. In the beginning, and in the Garden of Eden, Eve ate the forbidden fruit and exposed human race to problem. As a result of disobedience to God's command, God cursed human race and covenant of fatherhood was broken. Why? Because Adam and Eve went against instruction "Thou shall not eat a particular fruit in the garden" Their mouths served as gateway to the forbidden fruit.

Mouth is the channel through which the heart pours out its deposits. It is the radio outlet of the body. It is the talking drum of the body. But then, being a talking drum is not a license to talk anyhow and everywhere. You must exercise caution of where you talk, why you talk, how and when you talk. Let everything you say be moderate as you pick right word and make right statement. It is when you do this, you can claim that, your head is not for sale.

Tongue play major role in talks. The tongue is a small part of the body that can ruin or make us. The tongue is the control tower of the mouth. If you control the tongue, then you have protection, but if your tongue gets out of control and you are not a master of your words, the end is ruin. The book of ***Proverbs 21:23 says, "He who guards his mouth and his tongue keeps himself from calamity".*** The area you must protect is your mouth and tongue. To do this, signifies you are saying "My head and destiny is not for sale".

Many get filled and blessed, but fail to maintain it as a result of the tongue. You must keep a tight rein on your tongue if you want to contain the blessing of the Lord. It is one thing to be blessed; it is a different thing to contain it. If you use your tongue properly, it will be a tree of life you will feed from. We all eat the fruit of our tongue. If the fruit is sweet, you eat sweet fruit, if the fruit is bitter, you feed on bitter fruit. I pray that your mouth shall not sell you to bitter fruit. Claim it, that your head shall not be sold to bitterness. The end may be bad, it is death.

When God looks at our tongues, he forms estimate of our true spiritual condition. The state of your tongue is a very sure guide to your spiritual condition. The kind of words that come out of your mouth will indicate the condition of your heart. When someone says your heart is clean or dirty, he or she is referring to the state of your tongue. If the heart is good, the words that come from the mouth is good, we know that the heart is good. If the heart is bad, the words that come from the mouth are evil; we know that the heart is evil. You cannot have bad fruit from a good tree, nor can you have good fruit from a bad tree. There is deep relationship between the state of the heart and the state of the mouth.

By the words we speak, we create with words of mouth, and can as well destroy with it. Words of mouth can lead to quarrel, confusion or war; it can as well lead to understanding and peace. There is no war without an exchange of words. When quarrel, misunderstanding, strife, fight or war breaks out, souls may be lost. Quarrel and fight can lead to one party to seek powers to outdo the other party. Little quarrel of careless talk may go out of manage, that leads to witchcraft attack or sudden death. When you say, "My head is not for sale", it means, you are a manager of words you are loaded with wisdom It means you the type that avoid grape vine but say what is right and stand by it. It means you don't hurt with words of mouth.

What happens in life is as a result of our speech word. If there is going to be war, it starts with a word and if there is going to be peace, words must be involved. Mouth serves as outlet for all words. You can deliver yourself with words or bind yourself with one. In the beginning God created with spoken words, **"And God said, "Let there be light and there was light".** Genesis 1:3.

In the case of Paul and Silas, they sang and pray, and experience deliverance from the hook of untimely death. It was done by mouth. You can therefore use your mouth to wave death aside.

If you want peace know how and where you talk, when to talk, and when to be silent. What we say are powerful. We must mind what we say and where we say it, so that we don't speak our destiny into the hands of enemy. By this, don't announce when you are expecting good things or great harvest. By keeping quiet, you will keep yourself out of trouble, and out of agents that lurk around. They gather information to nail you. Don't answer questions from people without deep thought. Enemies are watching, this may be the point of your breakthrough. The question you answer may make you lose out, why?, because your mouth reveals your destiny to wrong hands.

When the Bible says, "Open your mouth wide and I will fill it", it talks of wisdom and understanding that will fill your mouth. When you open your mouth wide for God to fill it, your story will change. You will be loaded and re-loaded with heavenly treasures. The Lord will re-write your story and you will never fail. It is as if you declare, "My head is not for sale".

Joshua and Caleb brought deliverance to themselves with words of mouth. They escape wrath of God as a result of good report they established of the Promised Land. They won the day with mouth.

The mouth of the Phoenician woman brought her deliverance before Jesus, when she answered, 'even the dog eats what fell from the master's table'. Thus, there is power and joy in what we say. What we say matters a lot.

It is with mouth we pray, ask and speak good things

It is with mouth we sing to the Lord. **Psalm 40:3**

It is with mouth we speak wisdom. **Proverbs 10:14**

It is with mouth we speak great things. **Daniel 7:8**

It is with mouth we testify of God. **Psalm 89:1**

It is with mouth we reveal God's word. **Deuteronomy 18:18**

It is with mouth we reveal what is in the heart. ***Matthew 12:34-35***

It is with mouth we speak words. ***Psalm 19:14***

It is with mouth we laugh with joy. ***Psalm 126:2***

It is with mouth we eat. ***1 Samuel 14:26-27***

It is with mouth we drink. ***Judges 7:6***

It is with mouth we kiss. ***Songs of Solomon 1:2***

As good as mouth is, it is an outlet with responsibility. What it should do and what it should not do. The manner and ways you take to the do(s) and don't of the mouth tell who you are. Before you can claim that your head is not for sale, you must know the rules that guide your mouth. Hence:

- Use your mouth to speak what is true and just. ***Proverbs 8:7-8***
- Use your mouth to speak what is wise. ***Psalm 37:30***

You should guide your mouth properly. What then should we keep our mouth from? They are many. The Bible gives us a number of guidelines

We should keep our mouth from sin. *Ecclesiastes 5:6*

We should keep our mouth from perversity. *Proverbs 4:24*

We should keep our mouth from flattery. *Proverbs 26:28*

We should keep our mouth from arrogance. *1 Samuel 2:3*

We should keep our mouth from lies. *Revelation 14:5*

We should keep our mouth from unwholesome talk. *Ephesians 4:29*

We should keep our mouth from curse. *James 3:9-10*

When you do all these, and stick to them, what you are saying is, "My head is not for sale". "My destiny won't go to the wind". "I shall see the face of the Lord in whatever I do". "My head shall not dwell in witchcraft coven"

I pray as you do this, and claim assurance thereafter; your life shall not remain the same in the name of Jesus. Amen.

Now let's pray.

PRAYER POINTS

1. My mouth shall not lead me to trouble, in the name of Jesus

2. Padlock of darkness against my mouth, break in the name of Jesus

3. My mouth shall not reject food of life, in the name of Jesus

4. My mouth shall not serve as gateway to forbidden food, in the name of Jesus

5. Esau's mouth shall not replace my mouth, in the name of Jesus

6. Thou talking drum of my life talk right, in the name of Jesus

7. My tongue shall not lead me to trouble in the name of Jesus

8. My mouth, invite protection into my life in the name of Jesus

9. My mouth, shall not reveal my secret to enemy, in the name of Jesus

10. My mouth, receive divine healing, in the name of Jesus

11. Warfare, as a result of bad communication, end by fire in the name of Jesus

12. Witchcraft attack against my life, scatter in the name of Jesus

13. Power of sudden death assign against me, I bind you in the name of Jesus

14. I speak the word; evil shall not be my portion in the name of Jesus

15. My mouth shall not reveal my destiny to wrong hands, in the name of Jesus

16. Holy Spirit! I open my mouth wide fill it with words of wisdom, in the name of Jesus

17. My mouth, bring deliverance into my life, in the name of Jesus

18. My mouth, open wide for prayer, in the name of Jesus

19. My mouth, open wide, and speak words of wisdom, in the name of Jesus

20. My mouth, open wide and speak great things in the name of Jesus

21. My mouth, open wide, and testify what the Lord has done for me

22. My mouth open wide, and speak the word, in the name of Jesus

23. My mouth open wide, and laugh laughter of joy, in the name of Jesus

24. My mouth open wide, and drink fruits and wine of glory, in the name of Jesus

25. O Lord, keep my mouth from sin, in the name of Jesus

26. I put guard in my mouth against wrong talks

27. I am delivered, and promoted in the name of Jesus

For a better result and deliverance from witchcraft attacks, I recommend my books titled **830 PROPHECIES FOR THE HEAD** and **30 POWER POINTS FOR THE HEAD** to you Endeavor you buy them for sound deliverance and breakthroughs.

CHAPTER FOUR

FACULTY OF THE EYE

The eye is a pair organ of sight located below the forehead. It is one of the gateways of the body that transfer message to mind, the control room of the body. We see with the eyes.

Blindness refers to non-function of the eye. The eye is like a camera, taking picture of what it sees and store it in the mind. When the gate of eyes is open, lust can come in. This is the reason; you should close the gate of your eye against evil, in order to see kingdom of God.

A CASE STUDY

Our eyes being an organ of sight should not be allowed to go blind in the spirit or in the physical. When we say, someone is blind in the spirit; it means he can't see what others who are in spirit can see. There are times God will open your eyes, to see what ordinary eyes can't see. You don't need to be a prophet or prophetess before God opens your eyes.

It rarely happens but to others it does. The latter are referred to as prophet or prophetess. When you are in a gathering and prayer is hot, God can open your eyes through revelation. When such happens, try as much as possible to pray more and ask God for the gift of prophecy

But then you must pray and guide your spiritual eyes from attack. There was this sister who can see vision and prophesy. Her prediction is always vivid and correct until one day when she pointed at a woman in a congregation and said, "Madam, you have three heads with twenty one eyes. You are a chronic and acidic witch. Repent or else you will die"

The woman did not quarrel, but smile and said, "Pray for me sister, I don't want to be in the camp of Satan, I love Jesus".

This sister thought all was over, until on the third day when she was attacked in the dream. In the dream she saw seven demons in a fierce mood. First of all, they mercilessly beat her up to a coma and plug her two eyes out. She screamed in the sleep and shouted as she woke up. End of the dream.

Brethren, the story did not end there. The question you may ask is, what happen to this sister later in life? Yes, she did not die or lost her two eyes in the physical, but was spiritually wounded. She felt pain in her two eyes in real life. The pain did not go, for about seven months as she nearly went blind. But then, she was not left alone. She lost her inner eyes, as she couldn't see vision again.

The lesson we can learn here is, we mustn't do a show off with what God give us, but apply wisdom. This sister was gifted but was not prayerful enough. That was why, the demons over powered her.

I pray, you shall not be molested by witchcraft power either in your sleep or in the physical. Amen.

Now pray these prayer points.

1. Any power, assign to make me blind, run mad and die in the name of Jesus

2. Any dark hand, stretched against me in the sleep wither, and die in the name of Jesus

3. Stronghold of darkness against me, break in the name of Jesus

4. Holy Ghost Power, resurrect my spiritual eyes in the name of Jesus

5. Every gang up against my vision, scatter in the name of Jesus.

The fact remains our eyes can lead us to righteousness or hell fire depending on the information it passes to the mind. When eyes get bad picture into the head, it brings danger that hurts. No wonder brother Job said, **_"I made covenant with my eyes not to look lustfully at a girl" Job 31:1_**

The function of the eye is not only to see, but to see far and wide. This is the reason it is located at the upper region of the head. God didn't make the mistake of putting it under the foot, on the feet, stomach; shoulder or in the hands, but on the head. As you grow, your eyes are carried along horizontally at the upper region of your height.

Be wary of what you look or watch. When you look or watch what you are not expected, to do, your mind will be polluted. What you look or watch at times determines how you sharpen or destroy your destiny, and or, what you add or subtract from your destiny. What you see may mislead, or warn you from acting wrongly. Our look is mathematical in nature. It depends on how we apply it.

There are four types of people you come across in the course of life. You meet people by seeing them, only the blind meet people by voice or touch. As a person, the first categories of people (i) you are expected to meet are people that add value to life. These are people everybody virtually need. The second category, are people that may multiply you, These are jet-type like of people. They move ones destiny forward faster than expected. They are the Lord sent.

The third category of people, are those that scatter life. They are negative scissors that affects life. They cause sorrow in the life of people. They are pillars of woes you will ever regret coming across in life. The fourth category of people you may meet are those that subtract from life. They are people that kill gradually. They are cancer in the body. They are the people called in Pidgin English, "Then see me, then laugh with me, but then they do me bad things".

From this analysis, know where you stand. Take statistics of your life, so that you don't reap failure. Your destiny stands on three legs; today, yesterday and tomorrow. What you saw yesterday affects today, while what you see today tells what you may do tomorrow.

Eyes attract goodness to life. The Psalmist says, *"I will lift up mine eyes unto the hills, from whence cometh my help. My help cometh from the Lord, which made heaven and earth." Psalm 121:1-2*

This is power of faith. How can a person lift up his eyes to the hills and receive help? It is faith in place. This is what is called eyes of faith.

MY HEAD IS NOT FOR SALE

It is with eyes of faith you look at your minimum and explode it to maximum. You push all odds aside and match like a champion to possess your possession.

It is with eyes of faith you match from valley to mountain top. It is with eyes of faith a jobseeker sees himself as an employee of a good company.

With eyes of faith you claim deliverance over poverty, and say, "My cup runneth over".

It is with eyes of faith, a tenant looks at himself and says, "Soonest I shall be a landlord". Before you know it, it is sealed in heaven.

It is with eyes of faith, a barren woman sees herself as mother of children. She sees women with children, and say, "My children shall sit around the table with me"

It is with eyes of faith a prayerful man roll away obstacles standing between him and success.

When you lift up your eyes to the Lord, you experience deliverance from the head to toe. The Lord keeps you save from all manner of problems. He keeps you from death traps of kidnappers that truncate destinies. He keeps you from troubles of poverty and hardship that sinks glory. He keeps you from trouble of spiritual injury, and every manner of attacks, all because you lift up your eyes unto the Lord.

When you lift up your eyes unto the Lord, your head is lifted up. Your career and calling explodes for good. You experience deep deliverance from all manner of bondage. You experience uncommon breakthrough, uncommon testimony and power of fruitfulness.

As good as the eye seems to be, it can bring bandwagon of problems. Do you remember the story of King David, when he was having a pass time in the balcony upstairs? His eyes saw someone. It was Bathsheba in the bathroom, bathing naked. The eyes that saw Bathsheba led to the death of Uriah, her husband.

The story went further to tell us judgment passed against David, the son he had through Bathsheba died while Israel as a nation shared in the reprimand; 'sword shall not depart in the house of David'. Today, Gaza strip knows no peace while Jerusalem is in the hands of Muslims! You can see evils that eyes can cause.

What about the spies sent out, to spy out the Promised Land? Their eyes deceived them. They saw the Promised Land as a good place that can be possessed, but saw giants occupied it. Their eyes deceived them to the status of a grasshopper. Their eyes engineered them to speak what irritated God. They eventually paid dearly for it. Only Caleb and Joshua stepped into Canaan land among the twelve, because they don't allow their eyes to deceive them. They saw, they conquer and occupy. I pray this shall be your portion in the name of Jesus. Amen.

There is a particular part of the eyes that may send thousands of women to where they less bargain for, it is called eyelash. Satan has made an inn road to their lives through this.

This day, women buy **artificial eye lashes** and fix it in their eyes. They approach professional beauticians to fix these false lashes. This is nothing but captivity. The fact is, every woman is born with eyelash, but they neglect it, rather they prefer to correct God. They question God on creation. It is as if they say, "Oh man, you are a fool, why give me this size of eyelashes. I can do better"

The question is, can men or women correct God? The answer is simply, no. it is nothing but satanic crusade against womanhood. In the long run they become fools in their acts. They encounter dangers as they fix false lashes in the eye. What could be the danger? **And what should be done?**

- The first danger is the **loss of natural eyelashes**. Those who use false eyelashes for a long period are likely to lose the natural eyelashes. A condition named ***traction alopecia*** might also occur. This condition has the extensions causing too much tension on the natural eyelashes follicles. If you are lazy and you don't remove your extensions before going to bed at night or use them for the entire week, taking them off and changing them, your eyelash follicles may weaken and become damaged, which may lead to permanent lash loss.

The second danger is, increased **eye sensitivity**. Eye sensitivity increases with the use of eyelash extension. If you have always been a victim of allergies or with sensitive skin, there is the high likelihood of having irritation, itchiness, and rashes on the eyelid skin where the extensions are attached. If the irritating substance is not removed immediately, your eyes may become more itchy and watery and your eyelids may swell up.

The third danger is **eye infection or injury**. The fact that eyelash extensions are foreign to the body, it can cause infection or injury if it gets into the eyes. Even when a professional does the fixing for you, it is not risk free. Injury can occur if the tweezers hits the eyeballs or if the glue or extension itself gets into the eyes. This may lead to eye soreness, pain and visual impairment or blindness if the injury is that serious.

Bacteria and viruses can accumulate on the extensions and under the adhesive. If these bacteria enter the eye; they can cause a number of infections, including conjunctivitis and sties, which can destroy vision.

The last danger to the eye is **spiritual attack called loss of vision**. In the spirit, what you do with your body matters to God. When you apply strange materials in your eyes, strange powers may take over your eyes. Artificial eye lashes are witchcraft materials; hence it will be almost impossible for such eyes to see vision, because your body can't serve God and mammon the same time.

FOOD, EYE DISEASES AND BLINDNESS

The fact is, what we eat either consume or liberate us. The common foods we eat and our dietary habits violate one of the fundamental laws of nutrition. A lot of food and drinks we consume on daily basis destroy the eyes given the inseparable link between nutrition and vision. Most foods we eat are acidic; they block proper absorption of oxygen and other essential nutrients. The eye sight is first to suffer. Acidic food impairs blood supply to the organs and tissues in the body particularly the eye.

To prove that our eating habit contributes to blindness, it is logical to ask question like, "Have you ever seen a blind bird, fish, monkey, antelope, cat or tiger before?"

Except animals are wounded by hunters, the eyes of eagles, monkeys, elephants, goats and lions sustain their vision throughout their life span. Yet, the super-vision of animals is not a product of extraordinary creation by God. Rather, it is as a result of eating in compliance with the natural laws of nutrition. Because of our poor eating habit, we contend with rising cases of eye diseases, visual impairment and blindness.

Let's look at a number of foods we should avoid to improve our sight.

Refined sugar: This has no nutritional value, yet it depletes the body stores of B vitamins and other nutrients critical to the health and functions of the eyes. It damage healthy cells and tissues in the body including cells in the eyes.

Artificial Sweetness: Many people have replaced refined sugar with artificial sweeteners like Saccharine, NutraSweet, Splenda for teas and coffee; consuming these sweeteners this is like running from frying pan to fire.

Fried foods: Regular consumption of fried foods cause vascular problem by weakling the heart and impairing blood circulation. In effect, fried foods deprive the brain and the eyes adequate blood supply, thus causing visual impairment that deteriorate as we age.

Ice water: Consumption of water is good for the body, the brain and eye as well. But indulging in ice water on daily basis is worse for the health of the eyes. By how, you may ask? Ice Water causes poor digestion, impair blood circulation and depletes the body store of B vitamins governing the normal working of the brain and the eyes.

Caffeine: Coffee and Caffeinated teas cause danger to the eye. They contain caffeine which dehydrate the body cells, raise blood sugar and blood pressure, cause brain dysfunction and deplete nutrients that ward-off the risks of night blindness, glaucoma etc.

Refined carbohydrates: Refined carbohydrates are stripped of fibre and other essential nutrients. When it is consumed on regular basis, it can lead to heart damage, cause fats in the blood sugar or chronic inflammation that triggers glaucoma.

Red Meat: Red meat is always in the news for bad. It can significantly increase risk of blindness.

Soft Drinks: Regular intake of soft drinks harms the eyes. It promotes development of diabetes, which is the greatest destroyer of the eyes.

Carbonated soft drinks cause water logging inside the body tissues including those of the eyeball.

Refined Salt: As good as salt is, dominating our home cooking, it weakens the heart, cripples blood circulation and causes acidity that harms eyesight.

Whatever you eat let it be moderate.

PRAYER POINTS

1. My eyes shall not go blind in the name of Jesus

2. Thou camera in my eye, you shall not die, in the name of Jesus

3. Every blockage against goodness of my eyes, expire in the name of Jesus

4. Every passage in my eyes, that allow bad picture into my eyes, close by fire

5. Arrows of darkness fired against my eyes backfire, in the name of Jesus

6. Spirit of lust in my eyes I cast you out, in the name of Jesus

7. Spirit of adultery in my eyes, I cast you out in the name of Jesus

8. Spirit of vengeance in my eyes, I cast you out in the name of Jesus

9. Spirit of murder in my eyes, I cast you out in the name of Jesus

10. Spirit of arson, in my eyes, I cast you out in the name of Jesus

11. Spirit of failure in my eyes, I cast you out in the name of Jesus

12. Spirit of disappointment in my eyes I cast you out, in the name of Jesus

13. Spirit of idolatry in my eyes I cast you out in the name of Jesus

14. Spirit of blindness in my eyes I cast you out in the name of Jesus

15. Spirit of cataracts in my eyes I cast you out in the name of Jesus

16. Spirit of glaucoma in my eyes I cast you out in the name of Jesus

17. Spirit of long-sightedness in my eyes I cast you out in the name of Jesus

18. Spirit of shortsightedness in my eyes I cast you out in the name of Jesus

19. Spirit of lazy eyes in my eyes I cast you out in the name of Jesus

20. Spirit of crossed eyes in my eyes I cast you out in the name of Jesus

21. Every manner of diverse diseases and weakness in my eyes I cast you out in the name of Jesus

22. Witchcraft materials in eyes I cast you out in the name of Jesus

23. Evil calculations in my eyes, scatter in the name of Jesus

24. Looks that bring pollution, be nullified out of my life, in the name of Jesus

25. My inner eyes reveal people that will promote me, in the name of Jesus

26. My inner eyes let me know people that will promote me, in the name of Jesus

27. My eyes, shall not defeat me in the name of Jesus

28. My eyes of faith open by fire in the name of Jesus

29. My eyes receive deliverance, in the name of Jesus

30. My eyes keep me from all manners of problems, in the name of Jesus

31. My eyes keep me from traps of kidnappers, in the name of Jesus

32. Spiritual injury in my eyes, be healed in the name of Jesus

33. My eyes, experience uncommon fruitfulness, in the name of Jesus

34. My eyes shall not deceive me in the name of Jesus

35. Every bondage in my eyes, break in the name of Jesus

36. My eyes, receive liberty from captivity, in the name of Jesus

For deep deliverance from captivity of the eyes I enjoin you buy my books titled, **830**

TELLA OLAYERI

PROPHECIES FOR THE HEAD and 30 POWER POINTS FOR THE HEAD.

CHAPTER FIVE
FACULTY OF THE EAR

The ear is an essential part of the body. It is the gateway to sound that feeds the sensory organ. Every mammal has two ears, one on the left side of the head, and one on the other right side of the head. It is the organ of hearing. We listen with our ear. This organ called ear has both spiritual and physical functions. The physical aspect of it relates mostly to hearing and listening. Others include recognition e.g. females pierce their ears to enable them put earrings on. But as a result of attacks from hell this day, men put on earrings as fashion.

The combination of human ear and brain is fantastic. Hearing enable us to determine loudness, pitch, and tone and to approximate the direction and distance of sound sources.

The frequency range of a healthy human ear is roughly 20 to 20,000 hertz, or cycles of sound oscillation per second. The most sensitive region is in the 1,000 to 5,000 hertz range.

Ear has spiritual link with God. He whispers and spoke to us and many in the past. When Holy Spirit speaks to us, it is from God. Ear represents the tabernacle of God's voice. Most divine directives and instructions are taken with the aid of ear. Learning is taken with ear. When your ear is sound, your body will be sound as well. It is at this point, you claim, "My head is not for sale". You find yourself doing right thing at the right time. This makes you excel in life.

Spiritual link with God through the ear is good. Ear is special and spiritual. What your ear does to your soul and body may affect you. It is dangerous for ear to be under attack. When God wanted to call Samuel to service, his ear played major role. What he heard, Eli didn't. The conversion of Paul on his way to Damascus was incomplete without the mention of his ear. His eyes were gone, at least for a while, yet he got message through his ears. His conversation with Jesus saved him, as he heard every word spoken by Jesus. It was ear that played most of the role that day. I pray you shall not lose your hearing when God needs you. Amen.

Ear stands out as special organ of the body. Its uses abound and can be classified as follows:

Ear is used primarily for hearing. *2Samuel 7:22*

Ear is used to acquire wisdom and knowledge **Proverbs 2:2**

Ear is used to wear earrings, even though Christians are not encouraged to do so. **Genesis 35:4**

Ear is used to designate, by piercing a servant. ***Exodus 21:6***

Ear can be classified into seven areas, depending on how you apply them to circumstances.

1. There is ear eager to listen to Jesus. ***Matthew 11:15***

2. There is ear eager to listen to the Holy Spirit. ***Revelation 2:7***

3. There is understanding ear. ***Job 13:1***

4. There is deaf ear ***Isaiah. 43:3***

5. There is closed ear. ***Jeremiah 6:10***

6. There is uncircumcised ear. ***Acts of Apostle 7:51***

7. There is ear itching to hear falsehood. ***2Timothy 4:3***

YOUR EAR AND MUSIC

Ear is the organ of hearing, meant to listen to people's conversation. What we listen to will have influence in our life. It can make us, or destroy us. It can shape us or make us go astray. It can make us dwell in the valley or promote us to the mountain top. Music has strength in itself. This is why we must be careful of the music we listen to.

Most music this day is rubbish and is influenced from the pit of hell. They are mostly about lust, immorality and inordinate ambition. Terrible, senseless and lustful music sell most this day. This is what the ear is fed with. Ear accepts it, manufacture illicit out of it and pollutes righteousness in us. The fact is, as righteousness commeth by hearing, evil commeth by hearing too. This is the reason Christians should not listen to what may pollute or destroy them.

YOUR EAR AND DREAM

What then are the spiritual and physical implications of dreams that relate to ear? It is good to know this, so that we might handle every dream situation well. Every dream that relates to ear should be rightly analyzed and interpreted. Let's treat a number of dreams that affects the ear below.

- To dream of other people's ear suggests you shall hear surprise news.
- To experience an ache ear in the dream suggests a warning to look out for an untrustworthy person in your immediate circle.
- To dream of a very large ear suggests you will get help from unexpected source
- To dream of a very small ear foretells you will soon discover a false friend.

For detail understanding, I advise you buy my book on dream titled **DICTIONARY OF DREAMS**. It has over **ten thousand dreams and interpretations.** It is good for every home as a point of reference, when it comes to dreams and their interpretations.

Above all, what you feed your ear with determines your destiny. When you listen to good things and abide by them, you shall experience greatness. When you refuse to take to good counsel, you hear, you shall harvest failure. Invariably, when you claim, "My head is not for sale", what you are saying in essence is, "My ear shall not deceive me". "My ear shall not bury my talent". "My ear shall bring greatness to my life".

It will be of great help if we pray and claim our right, pray and be set free from what may captivate us. You need prayer to deliver your ear by fire, to anoint your ear for greatness and possess your possession. Hence, it is time for us to pray.

Now let's pray.

PRAYER POINTS

1. Lord Jesus, anoint my ear for signs and wonders in the name of Jesus

2. My ear receive deliverance, in the name of Jesus

3. I pull out evil plug in my ear, in the name of Jesus

4. My hearing shall not fail, in the name of Jesus

5. I pull out dark plug blocking my ear, in the name of Jesus

6. Every dark covenant with my ear, break in the name of Jesus

7. I soak my ear with blood of Jesus

8. Fire of deliverance heal my ear in the name of Jesus

9. Every vein in my ear be healed in the name of Jesus

10. Every evil vein in my ear work well in the name of Jesus

11. Evil padlock assign against my ear, break to pieces, in the name of Jesus

12. Every dark hand assign to slap me in the spirit wither, in the name of Jesus

13. Dark spirit assign to harm me in my sleep, die in the name of Jesus

14. Power of deliverance, deliver my ear from evil grip, in the name of Jesus

15. Witchcraft market in charge of my ear catch fire and roast to ashes, in the name of Jesus

16. Wicked injection against my ear, die in the name of Jesus

17. My hearing ability shall not be polluted in the name of Jesus

18. My father and my God, speak deliverance to my ear in the name of Jesus

19. My father and my God, speak success to my ear, in the name of Jesus

20. My father and my God, speak fruitfulness to my ear, in the name of Jesus

21. I shall learn and succeed with my ear, in the name of Jesus

22. My spiritual link with God shall not break in the name of Jesus

23. My ear receive wisdom and knowledge, in the name of Jesus

24. Dark earrings in my ear break to pieces in the name of Jesus

25. Physical earrings assign to lead me to hell fire; I reject you by fire in the name of Jesus

26. Killers of destiny quit my life in the name of Jesus

27. Heavenly anointing locate my ears in the name of Jesus

28. I shall not listen to what shall send me to hell fire in the name of Jesus

29. Dark puss, quit my ear in the name of Jesus.

CHAPTER SIX
WHEN THE HEAD NEEDS DELIVERANCE

Our head is not created for evil neither was it designed for failure. It is meant to generate ideas, purpose, research and development, to invent and to create. The head is a storehouse of breakthroughs and joy. It is the Centre point of existence, close to breathe. Air passes into the body through the nostril located in the head, and without breathe we are dead.

The head is a delicate part of the body, and should be handled with care. We mustn't allow it come close to failure or hit speed pump in the race of life. The head is created to create wealth not loss. This is the paramount reason we must not allow it to be controlled or supervised by contrary powers or manmade problems.

There are people who wake hale and healthy to life without the pre-knowledge that their heads have been sold in the spirit. They wake full to life and of hope for the day. They think of what to do, contracts to give or win, helps to render or receive from people; projects to execute or execute for them; merriments to prepare for etc., but suddenly situation changes. It takes different shape from what they plan. There and then, you heard reports of air mishaps, road accidents, armed robbery attacks and banditry, building collapse, terrorism etc. terminating their life. Once a soul is terminated, destiny is cut short of fulfillment.

What may have caused this, God or Satan? Every bad thing is traced to Satan, but at times, we use human wisdom that bring ugly dividend. Most times, it is said, "It is his or her star". Can this be true? At this point, I will like to answer this question with literary works of two great literary writers; **William Shakespeare** and **Ola Rotimi.**

We shall first answer it through the works of William Shakespeare in one of his books, **Julius Caesar.** "The fault, dear Brutus, is not in our stars, but in ourselves" From this, we can see that men create many problems only inviting Satan to make it robust. It is we that create problems through our thought. And as Ola Rotimi titled his play, **"The gods are not to blame"** More so, the Lord Almighty cannot be blamed for our wrong doing!

Beauty starts from the head. Your head is the storehouse of your destiny. Any embargo placed upon your head affects your destiny. Any embargo placed upon the head may cause struggle without result. It is witchcraft embargo placed upon the head that makes favour far from one. As such, helpers are scarce while doors of breakthrough refuse to open. When the head is under attack, good friends turn aggressive and unfriendly. It is therefore high time to declare war against every weapon fashioned against us to catch fire and roast to ashes.

It is a must to dedicate our head to God, not evil temples or shrines. Tell Jesus to lay hand of deliverance upon you. Your head must be a point of contact for God's works and human race. You should add value to life, be an asset to humanity and terror to Satan.

Any head under bondage needs deliverance from captivity. Satan and his agents have captured many through the head. Satan knew well one can be relegated to the background when his head is under attack. He attacks and prevails over his victims. He exercises dominion on the soul, when the head captured. He charge victims to spiritual court and condemn them in the spirit. The overall result is that victims live empty life as they experience constant failure at the edge of breakthrough.

Our head needs deliverance from possible attack of untimely death. Jezebel knew the role head plays when he warned Elijah that his head will not be on his neck the following day. Elijah didn't waste time but fled. When David fled the land of Israel in the wake of Absalom revolt, the life of Absalom came to an end when his head hanged among the tree. He died. Haman met his waterloo by hanging in the seventy five feet gallows, he prepared for Mordecia. His head went for it. When David defeated and killed Goliath it was by aiming at the unprotected forehead of the giant. He died and was beheaded.

In dark kingdom, the importance of head is well understood. Whenever they wanted to attack or kill a person they aim the head. They summon the head and cut it off with sword or break the head with rod.

When a head is severed or cut in the spirit it speaks volume.

When a head is severed in the spirit, it foretells termination of destiny.

When a head is severed in the spirit, it foretells announcement of obituary.

When a head is severed in the spirit, enemies rejoice.

When a head is severed in the spirit, it may announce end of a linage.

When a head is severed in the spirit, it foretells failure in the life of victim. He will end up a failure as he encounters one problem after another.
A beautiful destiny may have good stars but when the head is attacked the stars become useless. A star can be affected by star readers, by star highjackers, by evil pronouncement, or through bad name given to a child at infancy. Your name dictates your destiny and foundation.

The Bible says in the book of **Psalm 11:3, "When the foundations are being destroyed, what can the righteous do?"** When the mother of Jabez gave birth to him in pain, she named him Jabez meaning sorrow. For several years, Jabez lived in sorrow until he discovered himself through prayer and petition before God.

His head was tampered with on the day he was so named. He experienced deliverance, and head deliverance in particular the day God answered him. I pray your head shall experience unconditional deliverance by fire today, in the name of Jesus. Amen
Enemies can tamper with a destiny by laying evil hands on the head. Evil seeds are planted on the head, and when it manifests things become hard. Such victims struggle without result. This is the reason, you must pray against every form of pollution that may hunt you for destruction and eventual calamity.

It will be a help at this point to ask, what are the causes of head pollution? The answer to this can be enumerated as follows.

MY HEAD IS NOT FOR SALE

1. When herbalists make incision on a head and rub it with prepared powder or concoction, such head is polluted and needs deliverance.

2. When you use your head to carry one sacrifice or the other, during inter tribal war or boundary clash; or you carry one during festival or as a result of tradition; or you carry one as sacrifice to ward off sickness, it may result to head pollution. Such head needs deliverance.

3. When a man plaits his head or put on earrings, such head needs deliverance. There is what is called misrepresentation in law, you are misrepresenting yourself before God, and so, you must do necessary adjustment to pray for forgiveness and stop the act.

4. When your head is cursed, you need deliverance. No matter who cursed you, either it is your biological parents or not, you must break such yoke with prayer.

5. When you are addicted to drug, it will affect your brain and existence as well. Abuse of drug or use of hard drugs affects the brain, which is obviously located in the head region. When addicted in one drug or the other, your head needs deliverance.

6. When you don't pray at all, you can easily be manipulated by higher dark powers. Hence, you need deliverance.

7. When you visit fake pastors that wash your head in the stream or by river side, calling it deliverance, both of you are victims. You need deliverance, while he needs deeper deliverance, because he is a satanic doctor.

8. Your head needs deliverance, when you have persistent headache, or when objects walk in your head. This is an attack from dark powers that must be addressed. There are situations when the cap or head tie of a person is taken to herbalist to attack him or her. When this is done, the victim's head will be affected. It may lead to insanity, headache, pure madness or failure in life. Hence, he or she should go for deliverance because head is the focal point of life.

The next question that may be asked is; how can one know that his or her head needs deliverance? You can know this if you see yourself in any of the following situations.

    1. When unbelievers ask, "Where is your God?"

2. When surrounded by enemies, even when you do well.

3. When it seems nothing works for you.

4. When your head always swells up as if under attack

5. When your liability constantly swallow asset

6. When invaded with spiritual diversion.

7. When tears become daily routine in your life

8. When you fellowship with sickness and diseases as friends

9. When you are in constant sorrow

10. When you live in abject poverty.

Above all, take notice of your dreams. The head represents instrument of honour that brings increase and prosperity. The head is the reasoning faculty; hence it must be prevented from pollution in the dream.

Base on this, you must watch the dream that affects your head. Any dream that reflects attack on your head must be taken seriously and rebuked when you wake from sleep.

What are the dreams you should take notice of when dealing with issues that relates to the head. They are many, but you should address the under listed issues first.

1. When your head is shaved in the dream, mostly by unknown person, act fast in prayer, cancel the dream and claim your hair from evil hands. Your hair represents honour. It means your honour is under attack.

2. When arrow is fired at your head in the dream. Such arrow doesn't mean only the one fired at your head, but it becomes serious if your head was the target in the dream. The outcome may include insanity, untimely death, and failure at the edge of breakthrough. Cancel such dream when you wake from sleep.

3. When your head is severed in the dream. This is a dream that foretells calamity or untimely death, business doom or failure. Cancel it and claim your head back, so that your obituary is not announced prematurely.

4. When you dream your head is sold to strange people. This is a dream of destiny exchange that must be rebuked in totality.

5. When your head is broken with stone, coconut, rod or any strange object in the dream. It is a bad dream that can lead to insanity; business failure, backwardness etc. Cancel such dream by fire and speak woe to attackers of your life.

7. When your head is seen in the platter of plate in the dream. Pray against it, so that untimely death doesn't befall you, in the order of John the Baptist.

7. When your head is displayed as victim of war in the dream. It foretells arrow of untimely death in the offing.

8. When rubbed with evil object, concoction, evil soap or juju power on the head in the dream, it foretells evil manipulation upon your destiny.

9. When your head is tied with red or black bands in the dream, it suggests evil manipulation.

10. When you carry evil load on the head in the dream, it suggests carriage of evil load that may suggest poverty, sickness or failure in the offing.

11. When you dream of someone that calls your name with intention to harm you in the dream. It suggests, wicked powers are out to destroy your destiny. Pray fervently to counter such attacks.

At this point rise to situation, because many destinies are attached to you. When you fail to help such destinies, it shall be counted against you on the Day of Judgment. Hence, know at this junction that many destinies are waiting for you. If you don't fulfill your destiny, your father may not feel it, your mother may not feel it, but people you are expected to help shall feel it. But then, if you fail, God will look for a replacement, I pray, you shall not be replaced. Amen.

The question now is; what step can one take? The answer is simple. Take right step now and let it center on prayer and action. Pray the prayer of divine intervention. If God intervene in your situation things will change. Miracles will appear, signs and wonders will follow suit. Doors you felt are close before now shall suddenly open. Tears in the night shall suddenly turn to showers of blessing in the morning; bad dreams shall disappear in your sleep.

You who were once a victim in the dream shall suddenly defeat and kill powers assigned against you. Magic powers and juju shall fade away and become powerless for your sake. The gate of darkness that holds you captive shall suddenly open on its own accord, giving you way to freedom. Hopeless situation shall give way; why? Because there is divine intervention upon your life. There and then, you shall possess your possession.

When your head is delivered every other part of your body is delivered as well. Therefore, pray against powers of darkness that holds your head captive. Flush evil deposit in your head. Pray against bad luck assigned against your head. Fire back evil arrows fired at your head. Break every dark rod fashioned against you. Nullify every wicked pronouncement of the enemy against your head. Claim back anything enemies stole from you to cause failure in your life. Declare freedom for your head.

Today is today; let angels of God ascend and descend for your sake. Stop wicked powers from harassing you; stop them from every form of torments. Take bold step today, therefore, stop them before they stop you. Your head needs deliverance, and it shall be delivered in the name of Jesus. Amen.

Now let's pray.

PRAYER POINTS

1. My father and my God, direct me to the right place I should be at the right time in the name of Jesus.

2. Lord, give me good vision to discover myself in the name of Jesus

3. Angel of the living God; wash my head for signs and wonders in the name of Jesus.

4. Destiny quenchers assigned against my head die in the name of Jesus.

5. Powers of affliction against my head die in the name of Jesus.

6. Every power against my foundation die in the name of Jesus.

7. I flush my system of poisonous foods in the dream in the name of Jesus

8. Star killers!; release my star to me by fire in the name of Jesus

9. Any power that holds my head captive release it now in the name of Jesus.

10. Owner of evil load, carry your load and die in the name of Jesus.

11. Strange objects walking about in my head die in the name of Jesus.

12. I hand over, every bad luck gift in my possession to their owners in the name of Jesus.

13. I fire back, evil arrows fired against me in the name of Jesus.

14. Every dark rod fashioned against my head break to pieces in the name of Jesus.

15. Every dark stick fashioned against my head break to pieces in the name of Jesus.

16. Every curse pronounced against my head back fire in the name of Jesus.

17. Dark incisions on my head become useless in the name of Jesus.

18. Effect of evil sacrifice upon my head, die in the name of Jesus.

19. Effects of addiction on my brain die in the name of Jesus.

20. Every manipulation of darkness upon my life, scatter in the name of Jesus.

21. Every spiritual wash of the head that is now affecting me expire in the name of Jesus.

22. Every manner of sickness and disease on my head receive divine healing in the name of Jesus.

23. Any power assign to share my head die in the name of Jesus.

24. My head receive honour and glory in the name of Jesus.

25. Strange market! trading with my head, my head is not your candidate, catch fire and roast to ashes in the name of Jesus.

26. My head shall not be shaved in the dream in the name of Jesus.

27. I reverse every attack of the enemy against my head in the name of Jesus.

28. My head shall not be displayed as victim of war in the name of Jesus.

29. Every dark band around my head, break in the name of Jesus.

30. My head experience unconditional deliverance by fire in the name of Jesus.

31. My head fulfill the roles God destined for you in the name of Jesus.

32. Every embargo placed upon my head, break in the name of Jesus.

TELLA OLAYERI

YOU HAVE BATTLES TO WIN

TRY THESE BOOKS

1. COMMAND THE DAY

Each day of the week is loaded with meanings and divine assurance. God did not create each day of the week for the fun of it. Blessings, success, gifts, resources, hopes, portfolios, duties, rights, prophecies, warnings and challenges, are loaded in each day.

Do you know the language, command or decree you can use to claim what belongs to you in each day of the week? Do you know in Christendom, Monday can be equated to one of the days of creation in Genesis chapter one? Do you know creation lasted for six days and God rested on the seventh day? What day of the week can Christian equate as the first day of the week, if we follow Christian calendar? What day can we call day seven?

This book shall give insight to these questions. It shall explain how you can command each day of the week according to creation in the book of Genesis chapter one.

Above all, you shall exercise your right and claim what is hidden in each day of the week.

Check for this in **COMMAND THE DAY**

2. PRAYER TO REMEMBER DREAMS

A lot of people are passing through this spiritual epidemic on a daily basis. Their dream life is epileptic, having no ability to remember all dreams they dream, or sometimes forget everything entirely. This is nothing but spiritual havoc you need to erase from your spiritual record.

The answer to every form of spiritual blackout caused by spiritual erasers is found in, **PRAYER TO REMEMBER DREAMS.**

3. 100% CONFESSSIONS AND PROPHECIES TO LOCATE HELPERS.

This is a wonderful book on confessions and prophecies to locate helpers and helpers to locate you. It is a prayer book loaded with over two thousand (2,000) prayer points.

The book unravels how to locate unknown helpers, prayers to arrest mind of helpers and prayers for manifestation after encounter with helpers.

4. ANOINTING FOR ELEVENTH HOUR HELP.

This book tells much of what to do at injury hour called eleventh hour. When you read and use this book as prescribed fear shall vanish in your life when pursuing a project, career or contract.

5. PRAYER TO LOCATE HELPERS.

Our divine helper is God. He created us to be together and be of help to one another. In the midst of no help we lost out, ending our journey in the wilderness.

There are keys assign to open right doors of life. You need right key to locate your helpers. Enough is enough; of suffering in silence.

With this book, you shall locate your helpers while your helpers shall locate you.

6. FIRE FOR FIRE PRAYER BOOK

This prayer book is fast at answering spiritual problems. It is a bulldozer prayer book, full of prayers all through. It is highly recommended for night vigil. Testimonies are pouring in daily from users of this book across the world!

7. PRAYER FOR THE FRUIT OF THE WOMB

This prayer book is children magnet. By faith and believe in God Almighty, as soon as you use this book open doors to child bearing shall be yours. Amen

8. PRAYER FOR PREGNANT WOMEN.

This is a spiritual prayer book loaded with prayers of solution for pregnant women. As soon as you take in, the prayers you shall pray from day one of conception to the day of delivery are written in this book.

9. WARFARE IN THE OFFICE

It is high time you pray prayers of power must change hands in office. Use this book and liberate yourself from every form of office yoke.

10. MY MARRIAGE SHALL NOT BREAK

Marriage is corner piece of life, happiness and joy. You need to hold it tight and guide it from wicked intruders and destroyer of homes.

11. VICTORY OVER SATANIC HOUSE 1 & 2

Are you a tenant, Land lord bombarded left and right, front and back by wicked people around you?

With this book you shall be liberated from the hooks of the enemy.

12. DICTIONARY OF DREAMS

This is a must book for every home. It gives accurate details to about **10,000 (Ten thousand) dreams and interpretations,** written in alphabetical order for quick reference and easy digestion. The book portrays spiritual revelations with sound prophetic guidelines. It is loaded with Biblical references and violent prayers.

Ask for yours today.

For Further Enquiries Contact
**THE AUTHOR
EVANGELIST TELLA OLAYERI**
P.O. Box 1872 Shomolu Lagos.
Tel: 08023583168

FROM AUTHOR'S DESK

Authors write for others to digest, gain and broaden intellects. Your comment is therefore needed to arouse others into Christ's bosom.

I therefore implore you to comment on this on this book.

God bless.

Thanks.

CPSIA information can be obtained
at www.ICGtesting.com
Printed in the USA
LVHW081705030420
652141LV00009B/559